Seminar on the Acquisition of Latin American Library Materials

Bibliography and Reference Series, 23

This series is edited in the SALALM Secretariat, Memorial Library,
University of Wisconsin—Madison, Madison, WI 53706. Suzanne Hodgman,
Executive Secretary. Barbara Valk, Chairman, Editorial Board.

BIBLIOGRAPHY OF LATIN AMERICAN AND CARIBBEAN BIBLIOGRAPHIES

Annual Report, 1987-1988

Lionel V. Loroña, Compiler

PREFACE

With this year's issue, we have now reached the sixth annual edition of the
Bibliography of Latin American and Caribbean Bibliographies as a separately
published publication within the SALALM Bibliography and Reference Series.
Prior to the 1982/83 edition, the annual bibliography was issued as part of
the working papers of the annual meeting of the Seminar on the Acquisition
of Latin American Library Materials (SALALM). In arranging for a separate
publication, we hoped to make this file of important information more
currently available to all of us working in the field.

The true genesis of this publication, of course, goes all the way back to
Arthur E. Gropp's Bibliography of Latin American Bibliographies published
in 1968. Successive cumulative supplements have been compiled by Mr.
Gropp, Daniel Cordeiro, Haydeé Piedracueva and myself. These have been
published in 1976, 1979, 1982 and 1987.

As in all of these continuing compilations, the impetus behind them is the
work of the Committee on Bibliography of SALALM. The intent is to call
attention to recent bibliographies on topics of Latin American and
Caribbean interest. All bibliographies within the accepted subject range
(humanities and social sciences), and appearing primarily in 1987-1988, are
included. I say primarily since, as most of us know, there is often a time
lag in the reporting of a number of Latin American titles, and it is
certainly one of the prime objectives of this annual publication to note
this information whenever it becomes available. The entries are arranged
alphabetically under broad subject areas (or occasionally, by format).
Author and subject indexes provide added points of access. Bibliographies
appended to books or chapters of books, or to periodical articles, are
generally excluded. However, occasional exceptions have been made where a
bibliography substantial in volume or interest has been included within a
body of another work.

Once more I should like to express my gratitude to a number of people
without whose assistance this compilation would not have been possible: to
the members of the SALALM Committee on Bibliography; to Barbara Valk for
passing on to me all relevant items coming through the HAPI indexers; to
Nelly González, as Chair of the Bibliography Committee, and constant
contributor; and lastly, to Suzanne Hodgman and her staff for their
excellent job of editing the final manuscript and seeing it through to the
completed product.

Lionel V. Loroña

TABLE OF CONTENTS

GENERAL WORKS

1.   Abente, Diego. "Venezuelan Democracy Revisited," Latin American Research Review, XXII: 1 (1987) 225-240.

2.   Aguilera Peralta, Gabriel and Edelberto Torres-Rivas. Literatura en inglés sobre la crisis. San José, Costa Rica: ICADIS, Instituto Centroamericano de Documentación e Investigación Social: CRIES, Coordinadora Regional de Investigaciones Económicas y Sociales, 1986. 159p. (Para entender Centroamérica, 2).

3.   Arias, María Eugenia; Ana Lau; Ximena Sepúlveda. "Tabasco: una bibliografía comentada," Secuencia, 5 (May-Aug 1986) 87-111.

4.   Baver, Sherrie. "Puerto Rico: Colonialism Revisited," Latin American Research Review, XXII: 2 (1987) 227-230.

5.   Bibliografía chilena de obras en el exilio: lista parcial, 1973-1985. [preparada por el Comité Pro-Retorno de Exiliados Chilenos]: [revisada, ampliada y puesta al día por] Servicio de Extensión de Cultura Chilena, SEREC. Santiago de Chile: SEREC, 1986. 34 leaves.

6.   Blondel, Eaulin. A Select Bibliography of Material Located in the Library of the College of St. Louis de Gonzague, Port-au-Prince, Haiti: Prepared on the Occasion of the Assocation of Caribbean Historians 14th Annual Conference, San Juan, Puerto Rico, April 16-21, 1982. [S.l.,: s.n., 1982] 56p.

7.   Bunker, Stephen G. "Debt and Democratization: Changing Perspectives on the Brazilian State," Latin American Research Review, XXI: 3 (1986) 206-223.

8.   Calderón Quijano, José Antonio. El americanismo en Sevilla, 1900-1980. Sevilla: Escuela de Estudios Hispano-Americanos de Sevilla, Consejo Superior de Investigaciones Científicas, 1987. 375p. (Publicaciones de la Escuela de Estudios Hispano-Americanos de Sevilla; 326).

9.   Camarillo, Albert M., ed. Latinos in the United States: A Historical Bibliography. Santa Barbara: ABC-Clio, 1986. 332p.

10. Cardozo Galué, Germán, comp. Bibliografía zuliana. Ensayo 1702-1975. Maracaibo: Universidad del Zulia, Consejo de Desarrollo Ciéntifico y Humanístico, 1987. 483p.

11. Castro, María de los Angeles. Los primeros pasos: una bibliografía para empezar a investigar la historia de Puerto Rico. 2a. ed, rev., aum. Rio Piedras: Huracán, 1987. 130p.

12.   Centro de Documentación de la Gestión Gubernamental, 1982-1988. <u>Catálogo de documentos. Presidencia de la República, Unidad de la Crónica</u>. [México]: El Centro, 1984- .

13.   Chirif, Alberto. "'Monumenta Amazónica': fundamentos y organización de la obra," <u>Shupihui</u>, 38 (Apr 1986) 177-220.

14.   Clarke, Colin G. "Slavery and Dependencey: Studies in Caribbean Subordination," <u>Journal of Latin American Studies</u>, XIX: 1 (May 1987) 167-167.

15.   Colburn, Forrest D. "De Guatemala a Guatepeor," <u>Latin American Research Review</u>, XXI: 3 (1986) 242-248.

16.   Douglas, Daphne. <u>A Study on Public Documents in the English-Speaking Caribbean</u>. Paris: General Information Programme and UNISIST, United Nations Educational, Scientific and Cultural Organization, c1984. 104p.

17.   Dridzo, Abram. "Historiografía soviética sobre Grenada," <u>América Latina (USSR)</u>, 1(1986) 89-90.

18.   Dunkerley, James. "Central American Impasse," <u>Bulletin of Latin American Research</u>, V: 2 (1986) 105-119.

19.   Dutrenit B., Silvia and Martín Puchet. "Una bibliografía uruguaya," <u>Secuencia</u>, 1 (Mar 1985) 83-114.

20.   Enriquez, Laura Jean. "Half a Decade of Sandinista Policy-Making: Recent Publications on Revolutionary Policies in Contemporary Nicaragua," <u>Latin American Research Review</u>, XXII: 3 (1987) 109-222.

21.   Fenton, Thomas P. and Mary J. Heffron. <u>Latin America and the Caribbean: A Resource Directory</u>. London: Zed, 1986. [144]p.

22.   Figueredo, Danilo H. "Spanish Books [by Puerto Rican authors]," <u>Booklist</u>, LXXXIV: 2 (Sept 15, 1987) 116-117.

23.   Figueroa, Marie-Claire. "La inmigración intelectual española en México: evaluación bibliográfica," <u>Foro Internacional</u>, XXVII: 1 (Jul-Sept 1986) 132-153.

24.   France. Bibliothèque nationale. Departement des livres imprimés. <u>La littérature hispano-américaine publiée en France 1900-1984: répertoire bibliographique par Jean-Claude Villegas</u>. Paris: Bibliothèque nationale.=, 1986. 260p. (Etudes, guides et inventaires, 4).

25.   Gondard, Pierre et al. <u>Repertorio bibliográfico de los trabajos</u>
<u>realizados con la participación de ORSTOM: Ecuador 1962-1986.</u> <u>Repertoire</u>
<u>bibliographique des travaux réalisés avec la participation de l'ORSTOM:</u>
<u>Equateur 1962-1986</u>. Quito, Ecuador: Montellier, France: ORSTOM, Office de
la Recherche Scientifique et Technique d'Outre Mer, Institut Français de
Recherche Scientifique pour le Développement en Coopération, 1986. 69p.

26.   González Cicero, Stella María. "Siete libros yucatecos," <u>Historia</u>
<u>mexicana</u>, XXXIV: 4 (Apr-Jun 1985) 738-742.

27.   Graham, Richard. "State and Society in Brazil, 1822-1930," <u>Latin</u>
<u>American Research Review</u>, XXII: 3 (1987) 223-236.

28.   Grieb, Kenneth J. <u>Central America in the Nineteenth and Twentieth</u>
<u>Centuries: An Annotated Bibliography</u>. Boston: G. K. Hall, 1988. 573p.

29.   <u>Guía internacional de investigaciones sobre México. El Colegio de la</u>
<u>Frontera Norte. International Guide to Research on Mexico. Center for U.S.-</u>
<u>Mexican Studies, University of California, San Diego</u>. Tijuana, Baja
California: El Colegio; La Jolla, CA.: The Center, 1986- . Note: Merger of
<u>International Inventory of Current Mexico-Related Research</u> and <u>Estudios</u>
<u>fronterizons México-Estados Unidos</u>.

30.   Hilton, Sylvia L. "El americanismo en España: bibliografía, 1984-
1985," <u>Revista de Indias</u>, XLV: 176 (Jul-Dec 1985) 589-640.

31.   _____. "El americanismo en España: bibliografía, 1985-
1986," <u>Revista de Indias</u>, XLVI: 178 (Jul-Dec 1986) 655-732.

32.   Hughes, Roger. <u>The Caribbean: A Basic Annotated Bibliography for</u>
<u>Students, Librarians and General Readers</u>. London: Commonwealth Institute
Library Services, 1987. 71p. (Commonwealth Bibliographies, no. 6).

33.   Johnson, Peter T. "Facts, Statistics and Bibliographies," <u>Latin</u>
<u>American Research Review</u>, XXII: 3 (1987) 253-270.

34.   Kass, Scott. <u>A List of All Miami Herald Articles About Haitians,</u>
<u>1979-1983</u>. [S.l: s.n., 1984] 12 leaves.

35.   Lovell, W. George. "Voces desde la oscuridad: escritos recientes
sobre Guatemala," <u>Mesoamérica</u>, VIII: 14 (Dec 1987) 555-564.

36.   Merina Méndez, Ana. <u>Palma Sola--desde el sol, hasta el ocaso: un</u>
<u>aporte</u>. Santo Domingo, Dom. Rep.: Biblioteca Nacional, 1986. 152p.

37.   Moss. S. G.   <u>Books on the West Indies or by West Indian Writers: Held in the Richard B. Moore Library, Barbados</u>.   Barbados: Published by S. G. Moss, c1986.   127p.   (Richard B. Moore Library printed catalog, v. 3).

38.   Myers, Robert A.   <u>Dominica</u>.   Oxford, England: Santa Barbara, CA.: Clio Press, c1987.   190p.   (World Bibliographical Series, v. 82).

39.   Nickson, R. Andrew.   <u>Paraguay</u>.   Oxford, England: Santa Barbara, CA.: Clio Press, c1987.   212p.   (World Bibliographical Series, v. 84).

40.   Pagán Jiménez, Neida.   "Caribbean Books: A Bibliography," <u>Caribbean Monthly Bulletin</u>, XIX: 4/6 (April-June 1985) 19-21.

41.   Pérez, Louis A.   <u>Cuba: An Annotated Bibliography</u>.   New York: Greenwood Press, 1988.   301p.   (Bibliographies and Indexes in World History, 10).

42.   Potter, Robert B. and Graham M.S. Dann.   <u>Barbados</u>.   Oxford, England: Santa Barbara, CA.: Clio Press, c1987.   356p.   (World Bibliographical Series, v. 76).

43.   <u>Publications and Theses from the Bellairs Research Institute and the Brace Research Institute of McGill University in Barbados, 1956-1984</u>. Holetown, Barbados: Bellairs Research Institute, 1984-1985.   52p.

44.   Querales, Ramón.   <u>Contribución a la bibliografía y hemerografía del estado Lara (1557-1983)</u>.   Caracas: Gobernación del estado Lara, Instituto Autónomo Biblioteca Nacional y de Servicios de Bibliotecas, 1986.   2 vols.

45.   Reber, Vera Blinn.   "Paraguayan Bibliography," <u>The Americas</u>, XLIII: 3 (Jan 1987) 360-362.

46.   Restrepo, Fabio et al.   <u>Spanish Language Books for Public Libraries</u>. Chicago: American Library Association, 1986.   169p.

47.   Reyes, Dámasa et al.   <u>Bibliografía sobre cultura, comunicación y educación popular</u>.   La Habana: Casa de Las Américas, Biblioteca José A. Echeverría, 1986.   27 leaves.

48.   Rovira Mas, Jorge.   <u>Costa Rica: Bibliografía comentada sobre su crisis</u>.   [San José]: Universidad de Costa Rica, Facultad de Ciencias Sociales, Instituto de Investigaciones Sociales, 1987.   64p.

49.   Sutton, Paul.   "Grenadian Callaloo: Recent Books on Grenada," <u>Latin American Research Review</u>, XXIII: 1 (1988) 133-152.

50.   Tulchin, Joseph S. "The Malvinas War of 1982: An Inevitable Conflict That Never Should Have Occurred," Latin American Research Review, XXII: 3 (1987) 123-141.

51.   Tutino, John. "Peasants and Politics in Nineteenth Century Mexico," Latin American Research Review, XXII: 3 (1987) 237-244.

52.   Universidade Federal do Espírito Santo. Biblioteca Central. Bibliografia comentada de obras capixabas. Vitória: Universidade Federal do Espírito Santo; Banco do Estado do Espírito Santo; Aracruz Celulose, 1987. 159 [13]p.

53.   University of Florida. Libraries. Haitian Bibliography of Items in English and Creole. Compiled for the Latin American Collection, University of Florida Libraries by Robert Lawless. [Gainesville, Fla.]: R. Lawless, 1984. 115 leaves.

54.   Vasque, Josetine. Catálogo dos 854 títulos da batalha da cultura (Prefeitura Municipal de Mossoró, 1948-1973, Escola Superior de Agricultura de Mossoró, 1974-1983, Fundação Guimaräes Duque, 1978-1983): boletim bibliográfico, 153 números, Coleção mossoroense, série A, 25 volumes, série B, 414 plaquetas, série C, 262 livros: incluídos índices de autores e de assuntos. [Mossoró]: Escola Superior de Agricultura de Mossoró: Fundação Guimaräes Duque, 1983. 123p. (Coleção mossoroense, v. 259).

AGRICULTURE

55.   Bibliografia sobre agroindústria. Curitiba: Federação da Agricultura Estado do Paraná; Federação das Indústrias do Estado do Paraná, 1984. 25p.

56.   Bibliografia sobre tecnologias apropriadas. Brasília: EMBRATER, Serviço de Extensão Rural, Ministério da Agricultura, 1985. 115p. (Série bibliografias, 22).

57.   Elso G., Sonia and Veronica Bravo M. Bibliografía agrícola chilena. Vol. 7, 1985. Santiago de Chile: Instituto de Investigaciones Agropecuarias, 1986. Note: Vol. 1 published in 1977.

58.   Empresa Brasileira de Pesquisa Agropecuária. Catálogo de venda de publicações da EMBRAPA e de empresas estaduais de pesquisa agropecuária. Brasília: EMBRAPA Departamento de Difusão de Tecnologia, 1985. 78p.

59.   Empresa Catarinense de Pesquisa Agropecuária. Catálogo de publicações em estoque na EMPASC. Florianópolis: 1985. 20p. (Documentos. EMPASC, 45).

60.   Ferreira, M.T.R. and V. Naspolini Filho. Bibliografia sobre melhoramento do milho. Brasília: Empresa Brasileira de Pesquisa Agropecuária (EMBRAPA), Departamento de Difusão de Tecnologia, 1986. 2 vols.

61.   Kliemann, Luiza Helena Schmitz. "Fontes para estudo da questão agrária no Rio Grande do Sul," Estudos Ibero-Americanos, XII: 1 (Jul 1986) 115-124.

62.   Le Riverend, Julio. "Problemas de la formación agraria de Cuba, siglos XVI-XVII; comentarios finales; bibliografía general," Revista de la Biblioteca Nacional José Martí, XXVIII: 3 (Sept-Dec   1986) 155-196.

63.   Lista básica de periódicos em extensão rural: uma contribuição à acquisição planificada e cooperativa do Sistema de Documentação da Extensão rural, EMBRATER Serviço de Extensão Rural, Ministério da Agricultura. Brasília: O Serviço, 1984. 18[36] leaves.

64.   Monge, Claudia. Agroforestería tropical: suplemento bibliográfico no.1. Turrialba, Costa Rica: Catie, 1987. 210p.

ANTHROPOLOGY

65.   Bibliografía sobre medicina tradicional del Area Andina. La Paz: Instituto Internacional de Integración del Convenio Andrés Bello, 1987. 178p.

66.   Chaumeil, J.P. "Bibliografía Yagua II," Amazonía peruana, VIII: 14 (May 1987) 161-164.

67.   Chavarría Mendoza, María C. and José Cerna. "Fuentes para la investigación de la literatura oral de las etnias de la Amazonía peruana," Amazonía peruana, VII: 13 (Sept 1986) 161-175.

68.   Fernández Robaina, Tomás. Bibliografía de temas afrocubanas. La Habana: Ministerio de Cultura, 1985 [i.e. 1986]. 581p.

69.   Frank, Erwin H. "Bibliografía anotada de fuentes con interés para la etnología y etnohistoria de los Uni," Amazonía peruana, VIII: 14 (May 1987) 151-160.

70.   Hartmann, Roswith. "Medio siglo de estudios quechuas en la Universidad de Bonn," Revista andina, IV: 2 (Dec 1986) 607-614.

71. Holm, Olaf. "Bibliografía antropológica ecuatoriana," Miscelánea antropológica ecuatoriana, V: 5 (1985) 219-237. Note: Appears as a regular feature.

72. Jones, Grant D. "Recent Ethnohistorical Works on Southeastern Mesoamerica," Latin American Research Review, XXII: 1 (1987) 214-224.

73. Lozano, Eduardo. "Indian Religion and Mythology, Part I: Indians of Mexico: the Mayas and the Aztecs," Latin American Indian Literatures Journal, II: 2 (Fall 1986) 173-182.

74. _____. "Indian Religion and Mythology, Part II: Latin America (General), Central America and South America," Latin American Indian Literatures Journal, III: 1 (Spring 1987) 109-125.

75. Marino Flores, Anselmo; Juan Carlos Catalán Blanco; Roberto Cervantes-Delgado. Bibliografía antropológica del estado de Guerrero. Chilpancingo, México: Instituto Guerrerense de la Cultura, Gobierno del Estado de Guerrero, 1987. 328p. (Serie fuentes, 3).

76. McCallum, Janet. Folk Medicine in the Caribbean: An Annotated Bibliography. Kingston: Medical Library, University of the West Indies, 1985. 21p. (UWI Medical Bibliography, 36).

77. Monzon, Susana. "Bibliographie américaniste," Journal de la Société des Américanistes, LXXIII: (1987) 311-326.

78. Ortiz Hernández, María de los Angeles. "Bibliografía sobre pesca, cooperativismo y estudios extranjeros antropológicos sobre pescadores," Nueva Antropología, IX: 31 (Dec 1986) 177-178.

79. Ramos Guédez, José Marcial. El negro en Venezuela. Aporte bibliográfico. 2a. ed. revisada, corregida y aumentada. Caracas: Instituto Autónomo Biblioteca Nacional y de Servicios de Bibliotecas. Gobernación del Estado Miranda, 1985. 279p.

80. Rice, Prudence W. "Six Recent Works on the Maya," Latin American Research Review, XXI: 2 (1986) 228-237.

81. Vega Centeno, Imelda; Daniel Rodríguez; Blanca Cerpa. Bibliografía Aguaruna-Huambiza. Lima: Centro de Investigación y Promoción Amazónica, [198-]. 100p. (Documento, 8).

82.   Welch, Thomas L. and René Gutiérrez. The Aztecs: A Bibliography of Books and Periodical Articles. Washington, D.C.: Columbus Memorial Library, Organization of American States, 1987. 169p. (Hipolito Unanue Bibliographic Series, 3).

83.   _____. The Incas: A Bibliography of Books and Periodical Articles. Washington, D.C.: Columbus Memorial Library, Organization of American States, 1987. 145p. (Hipoloito Unanue Bibliographie Series, 1).

84.   Welch, Thomas L. The Indians of South America: A Bibliography. Washington, D.C.: Columbus Memorial Library, Organization of American States, 1987. 594p. (Hipolito Unanue Bibliographic Series, 2).

ART   AND   ARCHITECTURE

85.   Arte-educação no Brasil: bibliografia. [Organização] Escola de Comunicação e Arte. USP [e] Associação de Arte-Educadores do Estado de São Paulo. São Paulo: ECA: AESP, 1984. [10], 81p.

86.   Calderón Quijano, José Antonio. Bibliografía de las fortificaciones españolas en América en la Edad Moderna. Madrid: Comisión de Estudios Históricos de Obras Públicas y Urbanismo, 1985. 138p.

87.   Eder, Rita and Mirko Lauer. Teoría social del arte. México: Universidad Nacional Autónoma de México, 1986. 322p. (Cuadernos de historia del arte, 20).

88.   López Cervantes, Gonzalo. Bibliografía mínima sobre cerámica. [México]: Instituto Nacional de Antropología e Historia, 1986. 161p.

89.   Medina, Leticia. Catálogo del Archivo de Fotografías: colección edificios universitarios. México: Centro de Estudios Sobre la Universidad, Archivo Histórico de la Universidad Nacional Autónoma de México, 1984. 140p. (Serie Guías y Catálogos del Archivo Histórico de la UNAM, 8).

90.   Moyssén, Xavier. "Bibliografía mexicana de arte," Anales del Instituto de Investigaciones Estéticas, XIV-XV: 55-57 (1986). Note: Appears as a regular feature.

91.   Quirantes Hernández, Carmen Zita; Manuel Corcho Morffi; Isabel Serrano León. Bibliografía de arte cubana. La Habana: Editorial Pueblo y Educación, 1985. 346p.

92.   Loroña, Lionel V. A Bibliography of Latin American Bibliographies, 1980-1984: Social Sciences and Humanities. Metuchen, N.J.:   Scarecrow Press, 1987. 223p.

93.   _____. Bibliography of Latin American and Caribbean Bibliographies: Annual Report, 1986-1987. Madison, WI: SALALM Secretariat, c1987. 63p. (SALALM Bibliography and Reference Series, 20).

94.   Martínez, Julio A. "Fuentes bibliográficas para el estudio de la literatura cubana moderna," Revista interamericana de bibliografía, XXXVI: 4 (1984) 473-485.

BIBLIOGRAPHY (NATIONAL)

95.   Anuario bibliográfico ecuatoriano, 1984. Cuenca: Banco Central del Ecuador, 1987. 315p.

96.   Bibliografía mexicana. No. 12 de 1984. México: Universidad Nacional Autónoma de México, 1987. 179p.

97.   Bibliografia de publicações oficiais brasileiras, área federal: livros e folhetos. v. 5, 1985-1986. Coordenação geral, org. e. rev. técnica, Coordenaçao de Biblioteca, Seção de Recebimento e Controle de Publicações Nacionais. Brasília: Câmara dos Deputados, Diretoria Legislativa, Centro de Documentação e Informação, 1987. 671p. Note: v. 1 published in 1981.

98.   Biblioteca Nacional (Rio de Janeiro). Bibliografia brasileira. v. 4, no. 1/2-4, 1986. Rio de Janeiro, 1987.

99.   Biblioteca Nacional José Martí. Departamento de Investigaciones Bibliográficas. Bibliografía cubana. Jan-Feb 1987. La Habana: La Biblioteca, 1987.

100. Boletín bibliográfico. México: Agencia Mexicana del ISBN. Dirección General del Derecho del Autor, 1985. Apr-Jun, 1985- . Note: A monthly list of current Mexican imprints issued as a supplement within the periodical Libros de México.

101. The CARICOM Bibliography. V. 9, nos. 1 and 2, Jan-Dec, 1985. Georgetown: Information and Documentation Section, Caribbean Community Secretariat, 1987. 434p.

102. Catálogo ISBN, 1983. México: Secretaria de Educatión Pública, 1984. 175p.

103. Durón, Jorge Fidel. "Bibliografía hondureña en 1984," Boletín de la Academia Hondureña de la Lengua, XXVIII: 29 (Dec 1986) 95-107.

104. _____. "Bibliografía hondureña en 1985," Boletín de la Academia Hondureña de la Lengua, XXVIII: 29 (Dec 1986) 109-124.

105. Guyanese National Bibliography. Jan-Sept, 1987. Georgetown: National Library of Guyana, 1987.

106. Información bibliográfica. ISBN Bimestral. Buenos Aires: Cámara Argentina del Libro, 1988. Jan-Feb 1988. Note: A bimonthly list of current Argentine imprints issued as a supplement within the periodical Lea.

107 Jamaican National Bibliography. XII: 1-4 (1986). Kingston: National Library of Jamaica, 1986.

108. Kallsen, Margarita. Paraguay, dos años de bibliografía, 1985-1986. Asunción: [Cromos], 1987. 85p. (Serie Bibliografía paraguaya, 5).

109. El libro chileno en venta, 1985-1986. Santiago: Servicio de Extensión Cultural Chilena (SEREC), 1988. 246P.

110. Libros argentinos, ISBN. Producción editorial registrada entre 1982 y 1986. Buenos Aires: Cámara Argentina del Libro, 1987. 721p.

111. Libros colombianos. Feb-Dec 1985. Bogotá: Biblioteca Luis Angel Arango, 1986. 12p.

112. Martínez Capó, Juan. "Bibliografía puertorriqueña, 1984," Revista del Instituto de Cultura Puertorriqueña, XXIV: 88 (Apr-Jun 1985) 62-64.

113. _____. "Bibliografía puertorriqueña, 1984 (Continuación)," Revista del Instituto de Cultura Puertorriqueña, XXIV: 89 (Jul-Sept 1985) 72-74.

114. _____. "Bibliografía puertorriqueña, 1985," Revista del Instituto de Cultura Puertorriqueña, XXIV: 90 (Oct-Dec 1985) 61-64.

115. National Bibliography of Barbados. Jan-Dec 1985. Bridgetown: National Library Service, 1986.

116. Ramraj, Victor J. "The West Indies [1985]," Journal of Commonwealth Literature, XXI: 2 (1986) 137-147.

BIOGRAPHY (COLLECTIVE)

117. Biblioteca Pública Estadual (Alagoas, Brazil). Bibliografia de
autores alagoanos: levantemento das obras existentes na Biblioteca Pública
Estadual até 1984. Maceió: Secretaria de Cultura, 1985. 325p.

118. Giménez B., Cancio S. Escritores y músicos de la época de la Guerra
del Chaco. Asunción: Ediciones Intento, [1987-].

119. Hurtado de Jiménez, Luz, comp. Escritores de Antioquia. Instituto de
Integración Cultural. Medellín: Ediciones Autores Antioqueños, 1986.
664p. (Ediciones Autores Antioqueños, v. 21).

120. Millares Carlo, Agustín. Cuatro estudios biobibliográficos mexicanos:
Francisco Cervantes de Salazar, Fray Agustín Dávila Padilla, Juan José de
Eguiara y Eguren, José Mariano Beristáin de Souza. México: Fondo de Cultura
Económica, 1986. 462p.

BIOGRAPHY (INDIVIDUAL)

121. Aguirre Rojas, Carlos Antonio. "Bibliografía sumaria de los trabajos
de Fernand Braudel," Revista Mexicana de Sociología, XLVIII: 1 (Jan-Mar
1986) 309-313.

122. Alcina Franch, José. "Pedro Armillas (1914-1984)," Revista española
de antropología, XV: (1985) 323-328.

123. "Arturo Uslar Pietri: bibliografía," Mundo Nuevo, X: 35 (Jan-Mar 1987)
9-17.

124. Becco, Horacio Jorge. R.P. Pedro Pablo Barnola, S.J.: bibliografía
(1935-1983). San Cristóbal, Venezuela: Universidad Católica del Tachira,
1985. 16p. Note: Separata de la revista Paramillo, no. 2/3.

125. Berchenko, Pablo. "[España en el corazón:] bibliografía anotada[on
Pablo Neruda]," Araucaria de Chile, 40 (1987) 129-142.

126. "Bibliografía de don Bernardino Bravo Lira," Boletín de la Academia
Chilena de Historia, LII: 96 (1985) 47-51.

127. "Bibliografía de don Gonzalo Izquierdo Fernández," Boletín de la
Academia Chilena de Historia, LII: 96 (1985) 76.

128. "Bibliografía de Juan Benito Díaz de Gamarra y Dávalos," In: Moreno,
Roberto. Ensayos de bibliografía mexicana: autores, libros, imprenta,
bibliotecas. México: Universidad Nacional Autónoma de México, Instituto de
Investigaciones Bibliográficas, 1986, 13-34.

129. "Bibliografía de Leonardo Van Acker," Revista brasileira de filosofía, XX: 145 (Jan-Mar 1987) 56-62.

130. "Bibliografía del Dr. Robert Stevenson (hasta 1984)," Revista musical chilena, XXXIX: (Jul-Dec 1985) 58-79.

131. Bonavia, Duccio and Ramiro Matos Mendieta. "Edward P. Lanning y la arqueología peruana," Revista del Museo Nacional (Peru), XLVII: (1983-1985) 341-353.

132. Briseño Senosiain, Lillian; Laura Solares Robles; Laura Surez de la Torre. "Selección bibliohemerográfica de José María Luis Mora (1812-1850)," Secuencia, 2 (May-Aug 1985) 5-24.

133. Delgado Matos, Delbis; Ricardo Hernández Otero; Antonia Soler Mirabent. Bibliografía de José Antonio Portuondo (1932-1985): primera aproximación. La Habana: Academia de Ciencias de Cuba, 1986. 68 leaves.

134. Epple, Juan Armando. "Cronología biográfica y académica y bibliográfica de Guillermo Araya," Literatura chilena: creación y crítica, 24 (Apr-Jun 1983) 14-16.

135. Espejo Beshers, Olga and Ana M.R. LLoréns. "Pablo Neruda: A Selected Bibliography," Chasqui, XVI: 1 (Feb 1987) 83-95.

136. Fau, Margaret Eustella and Nelly Sfeir de González. Bibliographic Guide to Gabriel García Marquez, 1979-1985. New York: Greenwood Press, 1986, 181p. (Bibliographies and Indexes in World Literature, no. 7).

137. Ferguson, Stephney. "Marcus Garvey: A Guide to Sources of Information at the National Library of Jamaica," Jamaica Journal, XX: 3 (Aug-Oct 1987) 93-99.

138. Galanes, Adriana Lewis. "La obra inédita de Pedro Fernández de Pulgar en la Biblioteca Nacional de Madrid," Revista Interamericana de Bibliografía, XXXVII: 3 (1987) 369-376.

139. García Barragán Martínez, Elisa. "Diego Rivera: hemerografía indirecta," Universidad Nacional Autónoma de México. Anales del Instituto de Investigaciones Estéticas, XV: 57 (1986) 209-215.

140. García Carranza, Araceli. Biobibliografía de Emilio Roig de Leuchsenring. La Habana: Biblioteca Nacional José Martí, 1986. 2 vols.

141. Gaspar, Lúcia Maria Coelho de Oliveira. "Bibliografia de Gilberto Osório de Andrade," Ciência e trópico, XIV: 2 (Jul-Dec 1986) 203-218.

142. Gómez Martínez, José Luis. "Guillermo Francovich: una faceta de su pensamiento y un apéndice bibliográfico," Revista iberoamericana, LII: 134 (Jan-Mar 1986) 293-309.

143. González Boixo, José Carlos. "Bibliografía de Juan Rulfo: nuevas aportaciones," Revista iberoamericana, LII: 137 (Oct-Dec 1986) 1051-1059.

144. González P., José Antonio. "La tarea de un historiador del norte chileno: la obra de Oscar Bermúdez Miral, 1906-1983," Revista de Indias, XLV: 175 (Jan-Jun 1985) 213-224.

145. Haberland, Wolfgang. "Bibliografía de Franz Termer," Mesoamérica, VII: 12 (Dec 1986) 437-464.

146. Holguín Callo, Oswaldo; Félix Alvarez Brun; Graciela Sánchez Cerro. Bibliografía de Raúl Porras Barrenechea. Lima: Ediciones Clío, 1986. 126p.

147. _____.
"Bibliografía de Raúl Porras Barrenechea," In Porras Barrenechea, Raúl. Los cronistas del Perú (1528-1650) y otros ensayos. Lima: Banco del Crédito del Perú, 1986, 779-904.

187. Jackson, Richard. "Nicolás Guillén in the 1980's: A Guide to Recent Scholarship," Latin American Research Review, XXIII:1 (1988) 110-122.

149. Mamede, Zila. Civil geometria: bibliografia crítica, analítica e anotada de Joao Cabral de Melo Neto 1942-1982. Sao Paulo: Nobel: EDUSP; Brasília: Instituto Nacional do Livro: Vitae; Natal: Governo do Estado do Rio Grande do Norte, 1987. 524p.

150. Morales Saravia, José. "Alejandro Losada, 1936-1985: bibliografía comentada," Revista de Crítica Literaria Latinoamericana, XI: 24, (1986) 209-242.

151. Muro, Luis. "Bibliografía de José Fuentes Mares," Historia mexicana, XXXV: 4 (Apr-Jun 1986) 691-697.

152 Noguez, Xavier. "El Doctor Donald Robertson, 1919-1984: semblanza bio-bibliográfica," XXXV: 3 (Jan-Mar 1986) 511-520.

153. "Una nueva bibliografía de don Ricardo Donoso Novoa," Revista chilena de historia y geografía, 153 (1985) 43-56.

154. Paim, Antonio Ferreira. Alceu Amoroso Lima (1893-1983): bibliografia e estudos críticos. Salvador: Centro de Documentação do Pensamento Brasileiro, 1987. 60p.

155. Pellicer, Rosa. "Contribución a la bibliografía sobre J.L. Borges, 1973-1983," Anales de literatura hispanoamericana, 14 (1985) 190-215.

156. Perry, Larry Stephen. "Mario Vargas Llosa: A Checklist, 1952-1984," Bulletin of Bibliography, XLIII: 4 (Dec 1985) 235-247.

157. Ravines, Rogger. "Toribio Mejía Xesspe (1896-1983)," Revista del Museo Nacional (Perú), XLVII: (1983-1985) 333-340.

158. Rivas Dugarte, Rafael Angel. Fuentes documentales para el estudio de Mariano Picon Salas, 1901-1965. Caracas: Presidencia de la República, 1985. 207p.

159. Rodríguez, Celso. "The Writings of Lewis Hanke," Revista interamericana de bibliografía, XXXIV: 4 (1986) 427-451.

160. Román Lagunas, Jorge. "Bibliografía de y sobre Alberto Romero," Literatura chilena: creación y crítica, XI: 40 (Apr-Jun 1987) 27-30.

161. _____. "Bibliografía de y sobre Daniel Belmar," Literatura chilena: creación y crítica, XI: 39 (Jan-Mar 1987) 14-16.

162. _____. "Bibliografía de y sobre Manuel Rojas," Revista chilena de literatura, 27-28 (Apr-Nov 1986) 143-172.

163. Rubio de Lértora, Patricia and Richard A. Young. Carpentier ante la crítica: bibliografía comentada. Xalapa: Centro de Investigaciones Lingüístico-Literarias, Universidad Veracruzana, c1985. 222p.

164. Sabelli de Louzao, Martha and Ricardo Rodríguez Pereyra. "Bibliografía de Carlos Real de Azúa," Cuadernos del CLAEH, XII: 42 (1987) 129-138.

165. Santos, Vania Borges dos. "Jorge Luis Borges no Minas Gerais," Boletim bibliográfico. Biblioteca Mário de Andrade, XLV: 1/4 (Jan-Dec 1984) 189-190.

166. Schwartz, Jorge. "Oliverio Girondo: actualización bibliográfica," Revista iberoamericana, LII: 137 (Oct-Dec 1986) 1045-1049.

167. "Sessenta anos de ensaísmo literário, científico e artístico: colaboração de Gilberto Freyre em revistas nacionais e estrangeiras," Ciência e trópico, XIII: 2 (Jul-Dec 1985) 297-345.

168. Socarrás, José Francisco. "Bibliografía del Doctor Barriga Villalba, Antonio María," Boletín de historia y antigüedades, LXXIII: 755 (Oct-Dec 1986) 1149.

169. Torre Villar, Ernesto de la. "Wigberto Jiménez Moreno (1909-1985) y su bibliografía antropológica e histórica," Historia mexicana, XXXV: 2 (Oct-Dec 1985) 309-333.

170. Urbani P., Franco. "Bio-bibliografía del Ing. Alfredo Jahn (1867-1940)," Academia Nacional de la Historia (Venezuela). Boletín, LXX: 277 (Jan-Mar 1987) 101-145.

171. White, Clement A. "Bibliografía actualizada sobre Nicolás Guillén," Inti, 21 (Spring 1985) 145-163.

DISSERTATIONS

172. Caribbean: A Collection of Dissertation Titles 1861-1983. Ann Arbor: University Microfilms, 1984. 84p.

173. Corrêa, Carlos Humberto. Catálogo das dissertaçcões e teses dos cursos de pós-graduação em história, 1973-1985. Florianópolis: Editora da UFSC, 1987. 400p.

174. Volke Haller, Victor. Resúmenes de tesis de maestría y doctorado presentadas en el Centro de Edafología, Colegio de Postgraduados, 1961-1983. Chapingo, México: Colegio de Postgraduados, Centro de Edafología, 1984. 451p.

ECONOMICS

175. Alegre J., Lucy et al. Pequeña empresa y artesanía. Lima: Fondo del Libro: Banco Industrial del Perú, 1986. 206p.

176. Baloyra, Enrique A. "Side Effects: Cubanology and Its Critics," Latin American Research Review, XXII: 1 (1987) 265-274.

177. Bibliografía económica dominicana, 1978-1982. Santo Domingo: Banco Central de la República Dominicana, 1983. 125p.

178. Bibliografía económica dominicana, 1983-1986. Santo Domingo: Banco Central de la República Dominicana, 1987. 234p.

179. Bibliografía: estado y economía. Managua: Centro de Documentación, Instituto Nicaragüense de Investigaciones Económicas y Sociales (INIES), [1987]. 70p. (Colección Bibliográfica, no. 2).

180. "Bibliografía sobre políticas de ajuste," <u>Nueva sociedad</u>, 88 (Mar-Apr 1987) 199.

181. Calcagno, Alfredo Fernando. "Valoraciones del plan austral argentino," <u>Pensamiento iberoamericano</u>, 11 (Jan-Jun 1987) 425-432.

182. Carrillo Chaves, Mario Alberto. "La deuda externa de los países latinoamericanos pequeños," <u>Pensamiento iberoamericano</u>, 9 (Jan-Jun 1986) 417-425.

183. Chahad, José Paulo. "A evoluçao recente do mercado de trabalho no Brasil," <u>Pensamiento iberoamericano</u>, 10 (Jul-Dec 1986) 467-474.

184. Domínguez Villalobos, Lilia. "Las políticas de estabilización: el debate reciente," <u>Pensamiento iberoamericano</u>, 9 (Jan-Jun 1986) 425-430.

185. Dutra, Eliana Regina de Freitas and Yonne de Souza Grossi. "Historiografia e movimento operário: o novo em questao," <u>Revista brasileira de estudos políticos</u>, 65 (Jul 1987) 101-130.

186. Figueroa, Rethelny and Braulia Thillet. "Las empresas públicas en Centroamérica," <u>Pensamiento iberoamericano</u>, 10 (Jul-Dec 1986) 475-479.

187. Floyd, Mary Beth. "Examen de la bibliografía sobre integración económica latinoamericana (Translated by Delia Colombo de Puig and Elizabeth Teal)," <u>Mundo nuevo</u>, VIII: 29-30 (Jul-Dec 1985) 161-173.

188. Frambes-Buxeda, Aline. "Readecuación de la integración latinoamericana y del Grupo Andino al nuevo escenario mundial," <u>Pensamiento iberoamericano</u>, 9 (Jan-Jun 1986) 430-438.

189. Hartness, Ann. <u>Latin America and External Debt</u>. Austin: Benson Latin American Collection, The General Libraries, The University of Texas at Austin, 1987. 5p. (Biblio Noticias, 40).

190. Herken Krauer, Pablo Alfredo. "La economía paraguaya: una visión panorámica," <u>Pensamiento iberoamericano</u>, 11 (Jan-Jun 1987) 449-464.

191. Jordan, Anne H. <u>Economy of the Texas-Mexico Border</u>. Austin: Benson Latin American Collection, The General Libraries, The University of Texas at Austin, 1987. 6p. (Biblio Noticias, 34).

192. Lassanyi, Mary E. <u>Mexico and its Developing Agricultural Market, 1979-March 1987: 199 Citations</u>. Beltsville, MD: U.S. Dept. of Agriculture, National Agricultural Library, [1987]. 3, 21p.

193. Maduro, Acácia Maria Ramires et al. <u>Guia preleiminar de fontes para o estudo do processo de industrializaçao no Rio Grande do Sul (1889-1945).</u> Pôrto Alegre: Editora de Universidade, Universidade Federal do Rio Grande do Sul; Secretaria de Coordenaçao e Planejamento, Fundaçao de Economia e Estatística, 1986. 220p.

194. Mainardi, Stefano. "Empresas multinacionais na América Latina: a origem das empresas como variável interpretativa," <u>Pensamiento iberoamericano,</u> 9 (Jan-Jun 1986) 514-517.

195. Martner García, Gonzalo. "Estilos de desarrollo en América Latina: un nuevo debate," <u>Pensamiento iberoamericano,</u> 10 (Jul-Dec 1986) 509-519.

196. McClintock, Cynthia. "Capitalist Expansion and the Andean Peasantry," <u>Latin American Research Review,</u> XXII: 2 (1987) 235-244.

197. Miller, E. Willard. <u>Doing Business in and with Latin America: An Information Sourcebook.</u> Phoenix: Oryx Press, c1987. 117p. (Oryx Sourcebook Series in Business and Management, 3).

198. Munck, Ronaldo. "Labor Studies in Argentina," <u>Latin American Research Review,</u> XXI: 3 (1986) 224-230.

199. "As publicaçoes da Faculdade," In <u>História da Faculdade de Economia de Sao Paulo, 1946-1981.</u> Sao Paulo: A Faculdade, 1984. 2 vols. v.l: 517-611.

200. Palazuelos Manso, Enrique. "La economía cubana ante el rato de la industrialización," <u>Pensamiento iberoamericano,</u> 11 (Jan-Jun 1987) 486-496.

201. Potash, Robert A. "Investigando la historia económica de la República Mexicana temprana: escritos recientes y adelantos tecnológicos," <u>Historia mexicana,</u> XXXV: 1 (Jul-Sep 1985) 111-129.

202. Thiesenhusen, William C. "Rural Development Questions in Latin America," <u>Latin American Research Review,</u> XXII: 1 (1987) 171-203.

203. Topik, Steven. "Recent Studies on the Economic History of Brazil," <u>Latin American Research Review,</u> XXIII: 1 (1988) 175-195.

204. Walton, John. "Small Gains for Big Theories: Recent Work on Development," <u>Latin American Research Review,</u> XXII: 2 (1987) 192-201.

205. Waters, Paul E. <u>A Bibliography of Brazilian Railway History</u>.
Bromley, Kent, England: P.W. Waters & Associates, c1984. 30p. (Brazilian
Railway History Note, 1).

206. Weaver, Frederick Stirton. "Recent Scholarship on Industrial Growth
in Latin America," <u>Latin American Research Review</u>, XXI: 1 (1986) 173-187.

EDUCATION

207. <u>Bibliografía sobre educación en Chile</u>. Santiago: Oficina Regional de
Educación de la UNESCO para América Latina y el Caribe, 1985. 12p.

208. <u>Catálogo de publicaciones latinoamericanas sobra formación
profesional</u>. Montevideo: Centro de Investigación y Documentación sobre
Formación Profesional, Organización Internacional del Trabajo
(Cinterfor/OIT), 1986. 6a ed. 2 vols. Note: Includes items published
1977-1984.

209. Centurion, Mabel and María Julia Duarte. <u>Bibliografía de artículos de
periódicos sobre educación paraguaya, Año 1984</u>. Asunción: Centro Paraguayo
de Estudios Sociológicos, 1987. 119p.

210. <u>Financiamento da educação VI, Salário-educação: bibliografia
analítica</u>. Rio de Janeiro: Instituto de Estudos Avançados em Educação,
Centro de Documentação, 1985. 48p.

211. Instituto de Estudos Avançados em Educação. <u>Catálogo de pesquisas,
1985</u>. Rio de Janeiro: Centro de Documentação, 1986. 15 leaves.

212. Maestro, Gioia. <u>Bibliografía anotada sobre educación polivalente</u>.
Santiago de Chile: Oficina Regional de Educación de la UNESCO para América
Latina y el Caribe, 1986. 113p. (Serie bibliográfica, 1).

213. "Para seguir leyendo...," <u>Nueva Sociedad</u>, 84 (Jul-Aug 1986) 159.

214. St. John, Nancy and Audine Wilkinson. "A Bibliography on Literacy in
the Caribbean Area," <u>Bulletin of Eastern Caribbean Affairs</u>, XIII: 1 (Mar-
Apr 1987) 52-64.

215. Bibliografia folclórica, no. 12. Rio de Janeiro: FUNARTE, Instituto
Nacional de Folclore, 1987. 28p. Note: Each issue is a bibliography of
folklore materials. V. 1 published in 1977.

216. Travassos, Elizabeth. Catálogo das gravações do Núcleo de Música do
Instituto Nacional do Folclore: música folclórica e literatura oral. Rio
de Janeiro: FUNARTE, Instituto Nacional do Folclore, 1986. 111p.

GEOGRAPHY, CARTOGRAPHY

217. Alvarez, Leonardo. Bibliografía de trabajos de graduación sobre temas
geográficos: 1971-1984. Panamá: Universidad de Panamá, 1986. 33p. (Serie
Bibliográfica, 3).

218. Brazil. Diretoria de Hidrografia e Navegação. Catálogo de cartas
náuticas e publicações. Rio de Janeiro: A Diretoria, 1985. 65 leaves.

219. Ezguerra Abadía, Ramón. "Obras de geografía y ciencias afines de la
época de los descubrimientos en la Biblioteca Nacional. Adiciones,"
Historiografía y Bibliografía Americanistas, XXX: 2 (1986) 119-123.

220. Jordan, Anne H. Latin American Maps in the Benson Collection.
Austin: Benson Latin American Collection, The General Libraries, The
University of Texas at Austin, 1988. 6p.

221. Rodrigues, David Márcio et al. Brasil, A New Geographic Bibliography.
Belo Horizonte: Instituto de Geociências Aplicadas, Secretaria de Ciência
e Tecnologia do Estado de Minas Gerais: International Geographical Union,
Comissão Nacional do Brasil, [1986]. 266p.

222. Rumney, Thomas A. Mexico and Central America: A Selected Bibliography
on the Geography of the Region. Monticello: Vance Bibliographies, 1986.
42p. (Public Administration Series--Bibliography, P 1947).

223. Sarignana, Armando and María Cristina Sánchez de Bonfil. Catálogo de
mapas y planos. México: Sociedad Mexicana de Geografía y Estadística,
1986- . (Boletín de la Sociedad Mexicana de Geografía y Estadística, t.
138, v. 1-).

224. Torres Lanzas, Pedro. Catálogo de mapas y planos de México. [Madrid]:
Ministerio de Cultura, Dirección General de Bellas Artes y Archivos, 1985.
2 vols.

225. Aguilar Cerrillo, Edingardo and Patricia Salcido Cañedo. "Desde la microhistoria: referencias bibliográficas en torno a la revolución mexicana," Revista mexicana de ciencias políticas y sociales, XXI, nueva época: 122 (Oct-Dec 1985) 167-177.

226. Blázquez Dominguez, Carmen. "Siglo XIX y revolución en Veracruz. Una bibliografía básica," Secuencia, 6 (Sept-Dec 1986) 61-98.

227. Cadastro de cartórios do registro civil, 1981. Secretaria de Planejamento da Presidência da República, Fundaçao Instituto Brasileiro de Geografia e Estatística-IBGE. Rio de Janeiro: IBGE, 1982. 705p.

228. Campbell, Leon G., Jr. "The Historical Reconquest of 'Peruvian Space'," Latin American Research Review, XXI: 3 (1986) 192-205.

229. Constituinte: as eleiçoes das constituintes do Brasil-República. [Equipe, coordenação, Ivan Vernon Gomes Torres Junior; pesquisa, Ana Cándida Hack Teixeira Campos et al; catálogo, Adriana Moreno Silva et al]. [Rio de Janeiro]: Fundação Casa de Rui Barbosa, [1986]. 82p.

230. Even, Pascal. Guide des sources de l'histoire du Brésil aux archives du Ministère français des affaires étrangères. Paris: Publications de l'I.H.E.A.L., 1987. 63p. (Travaux et mémoires de l'Institut des hautes études de l'Amérique latine, 38).

231. Ezquerra Abadía, Ramón. "Bibliografía de México en la época colonial," Historiografía y bibliografía americanistas, XXX: 2 (1986) 79-123.

232. García, Alma M. "Recent Studies in Nineteenth and Early Twentieth Century Regional Mexican History," Latin American Research Review, XXII: 2 (1987) 255-266.

233. García Añoveros, Jesús María. "Don Pedro de Alvarado: las fuentes históricas y bibliografía existente," Mesoamérica, VIII: 13 (Jun 1987) 243-282.

234. Gilderhus, Mark T. "Many Mexicos: Tradition and Innovation in the Recent Historiography," Latin American Research Review, XXII: 1 (1987) 204-213.

235. Gómez-Martínez, José Luis. "Bolivia despues de 1952: un ensayo de interpretación," Los ensayistas, 20-21 (Summer 1985) 9-50.

236. Hampe M., Teodoro. "Estudios de historia del Perú colonial en revistas estranjeras, 1978-1984," Apuntes, 17 (1985) 109-125.

237. Lapa, José Roberto do Amaral. História e historiografia: Brasil pós 64. Rio de Janeiro: Pas e Terra, 1985. 110p. (Coleção Estudos brasileiros, 87).

238. Laviana Cuetos, María Luisa. "Movimientos subversivos en la América española durante el siglo XVIII: clasificación y bibliografía básica," Revista de Indias, XLVI: 178 (Jul-Dec 1986) 471-507.

239. Libros sobre la Revolución: 16, 17, 18 de julio de 1986, Auditorio Neysi Ríos, UCA. [Managua]: Escuela de Sociología, Universidad Centroamericana, [1986]. 48p.

240. Maciel, Carlos and Guadalupe Rodríguez. Breve reseña bibliográfica de Durango. Durango: Universidad Juárez del Estado de Durango, Instituto de Investigaciones Históricas, 1984. 276[14]p.

241. Matos, Odilon Nogueira de. "Documentos goianos," Noticia bibliográfica e histórica, XIX: 126 (Apr-Jun 1987) 111-120.

242. Matute, Alvaro. "Ediciones y conmemoraciones (Principales reediciones del Instituto Nacional de Estudios Históricos de la Revolución Mexicana con motivo de los 175 años del inicio de la insurgencia)," Revista mexicana de sociología, XLVIII: 1 (Jan-Mar 1986) 315-319.

243. McGowan, Gerald L. and Tarcisio García Díaz. "Independencia mexicana: bibliografía básica," Revista mexicana de ciencias políticas y sociales, XXI nueva época: 122 (Oct-Dec 1985) 125-160.

244. Mello, José Antônio Gonsalves de. Fontes para a história do brasil holandês: v. 2, A administração da conquista. Recife: Ministerio da Cultura, Secretaria da Cultura, 4a. Diretoria Regional da SPHAN, Fundação Nacional Pré-Memória, 1985. 506p. Note: Vol. 1 published in 1981.

245. Mora Rodríguez, Arnoldo. "Historiografía costarricense sobre el siglo XIX a partir de 1970," Revista de Filosofía de la Universidad de Costa Rica, XXIV: 60 (Dec 1986) 261-268.

246. Murray, David R. "The Slave Trade and Slavery in Latin America and the Caribbean," Latin American Research Review, XXI: 1 (1986) 202-215.

247. Neto, José Augusto Vaz Samopaio et al. Canudos: subsídios para a sua reaviliação histórica. Rio de Janeiro: Fundação Casade Rui Barbosa, 1986. 548p.

21

248. Nuñez García, Silvia et al. "Hacia una reinterpretación de la historia norteamericana: 126 títulos en bibliotecas mexicanas," Secuencia, 2 (May-Aug 1985) 104-170.

249. Oostindie, Gert J. "Historiography on the Dutch Caribbean (-1985): Catching Up?," Journal of Caribbean History, XXI:1 (1987) 1-18.

250. Quezada, Sergio, Arturo Güemez P. and Carlos E. Tapia. Bibliografía comentada sobre la cuestión étnica y de la guerra de castas de Yucatán, 1821-1910. Mérida: Libros, Revista y Folletos de Yucatán, 1986. 111p.

251. Salgado Moya, Clara. "La insurrección armada: Camilo y Che en Las Villas: bibliografía," Revista de la Biblioteca Nacional José Martí, XXIX: 3 (Sept-Dec 1987) 5-76.

252. Sarabia Viejo, María Justina. "Bibliografía de México en la época colonial," Historiografía y bibliografía americanistas, XXX: 2 (1986) 79-118.

253. _____. "Bibliografía de México en la época colonial," Historiografía y bibliografía americanistas, XXXI: 1 (1987) 121-168.

254. Scurrah, Martin J. "Military Reformism in Peru: Opening the Pandora's Box," Latin American Research Review, XXI: 1 (1986) 244-257.

255. "Les sources principales imprimées non-périodiques de l'histoire de Saint-Domingue de 1700 a 1789," Conjonction, 169 (Apr-Jun 1986) 155-157.

256. Walter, Richard J. "Vicious Cycles: Recent Works on Argentine History," Latin American Research Review, XXIII: 1 (1988) 153-164.

257. Weber, David J. "John Francis Bannon and the Historiography of the Spanish Borderlands: Retrospect and Prospect," Journal of the Southwest, XXIX: 4 (1987) 331-363.

INDEXES (GENERAL)

258. Ali, Shamin. An Index to the Research Reports of the Ministry of Agriculture, Lands, and Food Production for the Period 1971-1981. Trinidad and Tobago: Research Division, Ministry of Agriculture, Lands, and Food Production, 1984. 254p.

259. Eltzer, Bernardo A. Diarios nacionalistas en Argentina, desde el año 1940: bibliografía comentada de artículos sobre literatura y política. [Buenos Aires]: Ediciones S.J.L., [1986]-1987. 7 vols. Note: An index to the newspapers El Federal and El Pompero.

260. Indice de ciências socias, v.1, no. 7, 1987. Rio de Janeiro: Instituto Universitário de Pesquisas do Rio de Janeiro, 1987. Note: v. 1 was published in 1979.

261. Oleas Montalvo, Julio and Bruno Andrade Andrade. Indices de debates económicos del parlamento ecuatoriano, 1830-1850. Quito: Banco Central del Ecuador, Centro de Investigación y Cultura, 1985. 479p. (Fuentes para la historia económica del Ecuador. Serie indices de documentación, 1).

262. "Resúmenes de árticulos publicados en revistas latinoamericanas," Pensamiento iberoamericano, 9 (Jan-Jun 1986) 521-541.

INDEXES (SPECIFIC)

263. Chandler, Michael J. Subject Index to the 'Journal of the Barbados Museum and Historical Society', vols. 1-36. St. Ann's Garrison, Barbados: Barbados Museum and Historical Society, 1986. 56p.

264. Domínguez, Aleida. "Indice analítico 11 (Jun-Sept 1980-Dec 1985)," Santiago, 63 (Sept-Dec 1986) 145-213.

265. The Gleaner Index. National Library of Jamaica. v.1, no. 1, Jan-Mar 1986- . Kingston: The Library, 1986- . Note: Continues: AIRS, index to the Daily Gleaner (Jamaica).

266. "Indice alfabético de los números 1 al 8 de 'Mesoamérica'," Mesoamérica, V: 8 (Dec 1984) xi-xxxi.

267. "Indice de los primeros 100 números del 'Boletín del Archivo Histórico de Miraflores' del no. 1 al 98-100. I. Indice de autores de epígrafas; II. Indice de autores firmantes de correspondencia," Boletín del Archivo Histórico de Miraflores, XXIV: 118 (Jan-Jun 1984) 1-316.

268. "Indice de los primeros 100 números del 'Boletín del Archivo Histórico de Miraflores' del no. 1 al 98-100. I. Indice geográfico; II. Indice temático; III. Indice cronológico; IV. Indice de ilustraciones," Boletín del Archivo Histórico de Miraflores, XXIV: 119 (Jul-Dec 1984) 1-206.

269. Indice general de la revista 'Hoy'. [Santiago de Chile]: Servicio de Extensión de la Cultura Chilena, SEREC, Departamento de Indización, 1984- . Note: v. 1 indexes Jun 1977-May 1981. v. 2 indexes May 1981-Mar 1985.

270. "Indice 'Revista musical chilena', 1975-1985. Cuadragésimo año de publicación, 1945-1985," Revista musical chilena, XXXIX: 163 (Jan-Jun 1985) 73-155.

271. Merino Montero, Luis. "La 'Revista musical chilena' y los compositores nacionales del presente siglo: una bibliografía," Revista musical chilena, XXXIX: 163 (Jan-Jun 1985) 13-69.

272. Moreira, Maria Eunice. "Indice da revista 'Letras de hoje'," Letras de hoje, XXII: 70 (Dec 1987) 11-65. Note: Index covers 1967-1987.

273. Pauliello de Chocholous, Hebe. Indice de la revista 'La Escena', de Buenos Aires. Mendoza: Universidad Nacional de Cuyo, Biblioteca Central, Centro Bibliográfico, 1985. 129 leaves. (Cuadernos de la Biblioteca, 9).

274. Pérez Díaz, Máximo. Indice de la 'Revista social', (1916-1938). La Habana: [Ministerio de Cultura] 1986. 432p.

275. Rodríguez Rea, Miguel A. "La literatura peruana en la 'Revista ibero-americana' (Iowa-Pittsburgh, 1939-1985)," Revista de crítica literaria latinoamericana, XIII: 25 (1987) 191-235.

276. Rouse-Jones, Margaret D. and Annette Knight. "Cumulative Index, Volumes 1-19," Journal of Caribbean History, XX: 2 (1985-1986) 192-216.

INTERNATIONAL RELATIONS

277. Araya Montezuma, Andrés. "Material bibliográfico sobre el estudio de las relaciones internacionales en Centroamérica," Estudios sociales centroamericanos, 43 (Jan-Apr 1987) 93-106.

278. "Bibliografía sobre relaciones Europa-América Latina," Nueva sociedad, 85 (Sept-Oct 1986) 169.

279. Cochrane, James D. "Confronting Trouble in the Backyard: Washington and Central America," Latin American Research Review, XXII: 3 (1987) 196-208.

280. Domínguez, Jorge I. "Cuba in the International Aren," Latin American Research Review, XXIII: 1 (1988) 196-206.

281. Drekonja-Kornat, Gerhard. "The Rise of Latin America's Foreign Policy: Between Hegemony and Autonomy," Latin American Research Review, XXI: 2 (1986) 238-245.

282. Eltzer, Bernardo A. La armada argentina y el manejo de la opinion pública en los días previos al conflicto Malvinas, 2 de marzo-9 de abril 1982: bibliografía comentada. Buenos Aires: Ediciones S.J.L., 1987. 84p.

283. Ferris, Elizabeth G. "Interests, Influence and Inter-American Relations," Latin American Research Review, XXI: 2 (1986) 208-219.

284. Glasgow, Roy Arthur. "The Birth of an American Empire," Latin American Research Review, XXII: 1 (1987) 241-247.

285. Maríñez, Pablo A. Injerencias, agresiones e intervenciones norteamericanas en la República Dominicana: bibliografía básica para su estudio. Santo Domingo: Editora Universitaria, UASD, 1985. 28p. (Publicaciones de la Universidad Autónoma de Santo Domingo, 382. Colección historia y sociedad, 64).

286. Martz, John D. "Counterpoint and Concatenation in the Caribbean: The Substance and Style of Foreign Policy," Latin American Research Review, XXI: 1 (1986) 161-172.

287. Moraes, Joao Quartim de. "Brasil: a política externa da nova república," Pensamiento iberoamericano, 9 (Jan-Jun 1986) 452-455.

288. Moss, Ambler H., Jr. "The Panama Treaties: How an Era Ended," Latin American Research Review, XXI: 3 (1986) 171-178.

289. Nicaragua-United States Foreign Relations: A Bibliography. Monticello, IL: Vance Bibliographies, [1986]. 9p. (Public Administration Series--Bibliography, P 2031).

290. Nordquist, Joan. Current Central American-U.S. Relations. Santa Cruz, CA: Reference and Research Services, 1987. 68p. (Contemporary Social Issues: A Bibliographic Series, 5).

291. Ramírez Rivera, D. Rubén. "Hemerografía sobre las armas nucleares: una visión del armamentismo y el desarme nuclear," Relaciones internacionales, 36 (May-Aug 1985) 74-77.

292. Ray, James Lee. "U.S.-Central American Relations: Dilemmas, Prophets, and Solutions," Latin American Research Review, XXI: 1 (1986) 227-243.

293. Webre, Stephen. "Central America and the United States in the 1980's: Recent Descriptions and Prescriptions," Latin American Research Review, XXI: 3 (1986) 179-191.

294. Wolf, Ulrike. Bibliography of Western European-Latin America Relations. Madrid: Institute for European-Latin American Relations, 1986. 207p.

LANGUAGE AND LITERATURE

295. Allen, Richard F. Teatro hispanoamericano: una bibliografía anotada. Spanish American Theatre: An Annotated Bibliography. Boston: G. K. Hall, c1987. 633p.

296. Almoina Fidalgo, Helena. Bibliografía del cine mexicano. México: Universidad Nacional Autónoma de México, Filmoteca, 1985. 75[3]p.

297. Bansart, Andrés. El negro en la literatura hispanoamericana: bibliografía y hemerografía. [Caracas]: Equinoccio, [1986?]. 113p.

298. Bernd, Zilá. "Bibliografía específica sobre literatura negra no Brasil," Revista de antropologia (Brazil), XXIX: (1986) 175-183.

299. Bhalla, Alok. Latin American Writers: A Bibliography with Critical and Biographical Introductions. New York: Envoy Press, c1987. 174p.

300. Bibliografía de la literatura hispánica. Madrid: C.S.I.C., 1987. 207p.

301. Bibliografía del Instituto Lingüístico de Verano en Colombia. Meta: Editorial Townsend, 1987. 141p.

302. "Bibliografía: relación alfabética de los libros aparecidos y fechados desde enero a diciembre en España sobre literatura hispano-americana o temas afines," Anales de la literatura hispano-americana. Note: Appears as a regular feature.

303. Casimiro, A. Renato S. de. "Contribuiçao ao inventário do cordel juazeirense: I, Abraao Batista (continuação)," Boletim do Instituto Cultural do Vale Caririense, 11 (1984) 107-114. Note: Includes cordel published between 1977-1984.

304. O cordel no grande Rio: catálogo. Rio de Janeiro: Governo do Estado do Rio de Janeiro, Secretaria de Estado de Ciência e Cultura, Departamento de Cultura, INEPAC/Divisão de Folclore, 1985. 152p.

305. Focus on West Indian Literature: Booklist Prepared for the 14th Annual Conference of I.A.S.L. Kingston: Jamaica Library Service,[1985]. 45p.

306. García Saucedo, Jaime. "Cronología de la novela panameña, 1849-1985," Lotería, 360 (May-Jun 1986) 108-122.

307. Garner, Jane. Brazilian Novels in English Translation. Austin: Benson Latin American Collection, The General Libraries, The University of Texas at Austin, 1986. 4p. (Biblio Noticias, 36).

308. González Stephan, Beatriz. Contribución al estudio de la historiografía literaria hispanomericana. Caracas: Academia Nacional de la Historia, 1985. 214p. (Biblioteca de la Academia Nacional de la Historia. Estudios, monografías y ensayos, 59).

309. Gutiérrez-Witt, Laura. Latin American Cinema. Austin: Benson Latin American Collection, The General Libraries, The University of Texas at Austin, 1987. 7p. (Biblio Noticias, 39).

310. Harrington, Lucilia Maria Gondim. Relação das obras de literatura brasileira editas em inglês. [Washington,D.C.]: Embaixada do Brasil em Washington, Setor Cultural, [1987]. 12 leaves.

311. Jofré, Manuel Alcides. Literatura chilena en el exilio. Santiago: CENECA, 1986. 89p. (Serie arte y sociedad. CENECA, 76).

312. León-Portilla, Ascensión H. de., "Publicaciones sobre lengua y literatura nahuas," Estudios de cultura nahuatl, XVIII: (1986) 401-410.

313. "Listado de obras de teatro puertorriqueño publicadad entre 1800 y 1930, consideradas 'desaparecidas' por el Archivo Nacional de Teatro Puertorriqueño," SALALM Newsletter, XV: 2 (Dec 1987), 10.

314. Lobo, Luiza. "Literatura negra brasileira contemporânea," Estudos afro-asiáticos, 14 (Sept 1987) 109-140.

315. Long, Sheri Spaine and Kathleen Palatucci O'Donnell. "An Overview of Ph.D. Dissertations in Spanish and Portuguese at UCLA," Mester, XVI: 1 (Spring 1987) 64-69.

316. Lozano, Eduardo. "Latin American Indian Languages," Latin American Indian Literatures Journal, II: 1 (Spring 1986) 78-90.

317. _____. "Latin American Indian Languages," Latin American Indian Literatures Journal, III: 2 (Fall 1987) 225-234.

318. Luna Traill, Elizabeth. La investigación filológica en el Centro de Lingüística Hispánica. México: Universidad Nacional Autónoma de México, Instituto de Investigaciones Filológicas, Centro de Lingüística Hispánica, 1985. 56p. (Cuadernos de lingüística, 4).

319. Mancing, Howard. "A Consensus Canon of Hispanic Poetry," Hispania, LXIX: 1 (Mar 1986) 53-81.

320. Martínez, Martha. "Bibliografía sobre el teatro argentino, 1910-1934," Cuadernos hispanoamericanos, 425 (1985) 73-88.

321. Moisés, Massaud. "Selected Bibliography of Brazilian Literature," Chasqui, XV: 2-3 (Feb-May 1986) 48-78.

322. Muñoz, Willy O. "Teatro boliviano: la última época, 1967-1985," Los ensayistas, 20-21 (Summer 1986) 175-187.

323. Ordenes, Jorge. "El ensayo boliviano a partir de la guerra de Chaco," Los ensayistas, 20-21 (Summer 1986) 135-146.

324. Pascal-Trouillot, Ertha. "Bibliographie féminine de l'epoque coloniale e XIXe siècle," Conjonction, 169 (Apr-Jun 1985) 147-156.

325. Paz Soldán, Alba María. "Indice de la novela boliviana, 1931-1978," Revista iberoamericana, LII: 134 (Jan-Mar 1986) 311-320.

326. Ramírez, Juan José. Selección hemerográfica de autores monagüenses. Maturín, Venezuela: Biblioteca de Temas y Autores Monagüenses, [1985]. 331p.

327. Rela, Walter. Literatura uruguaya: bibliografía selectiva. Tempe: Center for Latin American Studies, Arizona State University, c1986. 86p. (Special Studies, 26).

328. Rivera-Rodas, Oscar. "La revolución de 1952 y la narrativa boliviana," Los ensayistas, 20-21 (Summer 1986) 147-160.

329. Rodríguez-Peralta, Phyllis. "Early Novels by Prose Modernists: Continuation and Transition," Revista de estudios hispánicos (Vassar), XX: 1 (Jan 1986) 59-75.

330. Schon, Isabel. Basic Collection of Children's Books in Spanish. Metuchen, N.J.: Scarecrow Press, 1986. 230p.

331. _____. Books in Spanish for Children and Young Adults: An Annotated Guide. Series IV. Metuchen, N.J.: Scarecrow Press, 1987. 301p.

332. _____. "Children's Books from Cuba: Dull and Dogmatic," Hispania, LII: 3 (Sept 1987) 655-657.

333. Siles, Juan Ignacio. "El cuento y la difícil coexistencia boliviana," Los ensayistas, 20-21 (Summer 1986) 161-173.

334. Trujillo, Roberto G. and Andrés Rodríguez. Literatura Chicana: Creative and Critical Writings Through 1984. Oakland,CA: Floricanto Press, c1985. 95p.

335. Verani, Hugo J. José Emilio Pacheco ante la crítica. México: Dirección de Difusión Cultural, Universidad Autónoma Metro-politana, c1987. 310p. (Colección de cultura universitaria, serie ensayo, 36).

336. Williams, Lorna V. "Recent Works on Afro-Hispanic Literature," Latin American Research Review, XXII: 2 (1987) 245-254.

337. Wise S., Mary Ruth. Bibliografía del Instituto Lingüístico de Verano en el Perú, 1946-1986. Lima: Ministerio de Educación: Instituto Lingüístico de Verano, 1986. 379p.

338. Woodbridge, Hensley Charles. Guide to Reference Works for the Study of the Spanish Language and Literature and Spanish American Literature. New York: Modern Language Association of America, 1987. 183p. (Selected Bibliographies in Language and Literature, 5).

LAW

339. Boletín hemerográfico jurídico. No. 1, Feb. 1985- . Xalapa: Universidad Veracruzana, Instituto de Investigaciones Jurídicas, 1985- .

340. Newton, Velma, Commonwealth Caribbean Legal Literature: A Bibliography of All Primary Sources to Date and Secondary Sources for 1971-85. 2nd. ed. Barbados: Faculty of Law Library, University of the West Indies, Cave Hill Campus, 1987. 492p. Note: This is a revised edition of Legal Literature and Conditions Affecting Legal Publishing in the Commonwealth Caribbean published in 1979.

341. Rosa, Maria Clementina. <u>Constitucionalidade das leis: bibliografia</u>.
Brasília: Supremo Tribunal Federal, Serviço de Documentação e Informática,
1986. 37p.

LIBRARIES AND ARCHIVES

342. Alanís Boyso, José Luis and María Antonieta Ruíz Nateras. <u>Archivalía
municipal del Estado de México</u>. Toluca: Gobierno del Estado de México,
Secretaría de Educación, Cultura y Bienestar Social, Dirección de
Patrimonio Cultural, 1985. 252p.

343. Archivo General de Centroamerica. <u>Documentos coloniales de Chiapas en
el Archivo General de Centroamérica</u>. Guatemala: Ministerio de Educación,
el Archivo, 1986. 63p.

344. Archivo Histórico Nacional (Spain). Sección de Ultramar. <u>Papeles de
Santo Domingo</u>. María Teresa de la Peña Marazuela; María Teresa Díaz de los
Ríos San Juan; María Angeles Ortega Benayas. Madrid: Ministerio de
Cultura, Dirección General de Bellas Artes, 1985. 379p.

345. Arquivo Histórico do Rio Grande do Sul. <u>Levantamento bibliográfico de
obras existentes no AHRS sobre Revolução Farroupilha</u>. Porto Alegre: O
Arquivo, 1985. 25p.

346. Argentina. Academia Nacional de la Historia. <u>Catálogo del archivo
Norberto Quirno Costa</u>. Buenos Aires: Academia Nacional de la Historia,
1986. 384p. (Biblioteca de publicaciones documentales, 18).

347. "[Atualização do acervo da Biblioteca Mário de Andrade]," <u>Boletim
bibliográfico. Biblioteca Mário de Andrade</u>, XLIV: 1/4 (Jan-Dec 1983) 149-
174.

348. Beloch, Israel. <u>Guia dos arquivos privados relevantes para o estudo
da história da política económica no Brasil, 1822-1964</u>. Brasília: IPFA;
Recife: ANPEC; Sao Paulo: PNPE, 1986. 252p.

349. Biblioteca "Emílio Guimarães Moura" (Belo Horizonte, Brazil).
<u>Mineiriana: relação das obras existentes na Sala Mineiriana da Biblioteca
"Emilio Guimarães"</u>. Elizabeth Manha Lacerda, Eda Marli Bellone Fonseca.
Belo Horizonte: Faculdade de Ciências Económicas, UFMG, 1986. 187p.

350. Centro de Documentação do Pensamento Brasileiro. <u>Catálogo do acervo</u>. 2a ed. Salvador: O Centro, 1985. 44p.

351. Chauleau, Liliane. <u>Conseil souverain de la Martinique, 1712-1791: inventaire analytique</u>. Fort-de-France: Archives Départementales de la Martinique, 1985. 400p.

352. Gianelloni, Julie et al. <u>Colección Especial Rutherford B. Hayes</u>. [Asunción]: Centro Cultural Paraguayo-Americano, 1985. 73p.

353. Hernández y Lazo, Begoña. <u>Guía del Archivo Jacinto B. Treviño</u>. México: Centro de Estudios sobre la Universidad, Universidad Autónoma de México, 1984. 68p. (Archivo Histórico de la UNAM. Serie guías y catálogos del Archivo Histórico de la UNAM, 7).

354. Mexico. Archivo General de la Nación. <u>Serie correspondencia de virreyes: marqués de Branciforte</u>. Elaborado por María Elena Bribiesca Sumano, Ariel Acevedo García, Moisés Pacheco Casales. México: Archivo General de la Nación, 1985- . (Guías y catálogos, 74).

355. _____. <u>Serie judicial</u>. Elaborado por María Elena Bribiesca Sumano, Luz María González Gómez, Victor Manuel Briseño García. México: Archivo General de la Nación, 1985- . (Guías y catálogos, 73).

356. Querales D., Juan Bautista. <u>Catálogo de documentos históricos del Registro Principal del Distrito Federal, 1630-1892: sección cajas negras</u>. Caracas: Academia Nacional de la Historia, Departamento de Investigaciones Históricas, 1985. 210p. (Biblioteca de la Academia Nacional de la Historia. Serie archivos y catálogos, 4).

357. Robinson, D. J. and Linda Greenow. <u>Catálogo del archivo del Registro Público de la Propriedad de Guadalajara: libros de hipotecas 1566-1820</u>. México: Gobierno de Jalisco, Secretaría General, Unidad Editorial, 1986. 256p.

358. Sánchez Pineda, Antonia C. and Margarita Menegus Bornemann. <u>Catálogo del Archivo Ezequiel A. Chávez: manuscritos y obras impresas</u>. México: Universidad Nacional Autónoma de México, Centro de Estudios sobre la Universidad, Archivo Histórico, 1984. 151p.

359. Schwartz, Jorge. "A bibliografía latino-americana na Coleçao Marinetti," Boletim biblliográfico. Biblioteca Mário de Andrade, XLIV: 1/4 (Jan-Dec 1983) 131-145.

360. Soares, Iaponam. Arquivos e documentos em Santa Catarina. Florianópolis: Arquivo Público do Estado, 1985. 127p. (Coleçao José Gonçalves dos Santos Silva, 1).

361. Sociedad Mexicana de Geografía y Estadística. Biblioteca "Benito Juárez". Inventario Biblioteca Benito Juárez. Miguel Civeira Taboada et al. México: la Sociedad, 1986- . (Boletín de la Sociedad Mexicana de Geografía y Estadística, 139-).

362. Torras Camacho, Norma. Suplemento de trabajos de archivo: trabajos originales que se encuentran en el Departamento de Documentación de la Subdirección de Servicios Científicos Técnicos del C.I.P.. La Habana: Centro de Investigaciones Pesqueras, 1984. 27 leaves.

363. Universidade Federal de Mato Grosso do Sul. Biblioteca Central. Catálogo de material bibliográfico sobre Mato Grosso do Sul e Mato Grosso existente na Biblioteca Central, UFMS. Ministério da Educação e Cultura, Universidade Federal de Mato Grosso do Sul, Pro-Reitoria de Assuntos Comunitários, Biblioteca Central. Campo Grande: A Biblioteca, 1984. 59 leaves.

364. University of Maryland. College Park. Libraries. Archives. Guide to the Cuba Company Archives. College Park, MD: Historical Manuscripts and Archives Dept., University of Maryland College Park Libraries, 1985. 12 [22]p.

365. Vizcaya, Isidro. El archivo del insurgente José Rafael de Iriarte. Monterrey: Archivo General del Estado de Nuevo Leon, 1985. 347p.

366. Vos, Jan de. Catálogo de los documentos históricos que se conservan en el fondo llamado "Provincia de Chiapas" del Archivo General de Centroamérica, Guatemala. San Cristóbal de las Casas: Centro de Estudios Indígenas, UNACH, Centro de Investigaciones Ecológicas del Sureste, 1985. 2 vols.

367. Weeks, John M. Maya Ethnohistory: A Guide to Spanish Colonial Documents at Tozzer Library, Harvard University. Nashville: Vanderbilt University, 1987. 121p. (Vanderbilt University Publications in Anthropology, 34).

368. Weis, W. Michael. "The Fundação Getúlio Vargas and the New Getúlio," Luso-Brazilian Review, XXIV: 2 (Winter 1987) 49-60.

369. "Catálogo dos manuscritos sobre o Rio de Janeiro existentes na Biblioteca Nacional, II: Século XIX (1801-1834)," Brazil. Biblioteca Nacional. Anais, 104 (1984) 1-170.

370. Rotemberg, Marisa. Catalogus librorum Musaei Goeldiani. I. Cimelia: catálogo descritivo das obras raras, séculos XVI, XVII e XVIII. Belém: MCT/CNPq, Museu Paraense Emílio Goeldi, 1987. 257p.

371. Schwaller, John Frederick. "Guías de manuscritos en náhuatl conservados en The Newberry Library (Chicago), The Latin American Library of Tulane University, The Bancroft Library, University of California, Berkeley," Estudios de Cultura Nahuatl, XVIII: (1986) 315-383.

372. Suarez Pasquel, Lucía. Fondo Neptalí Bonifaz. [Quito]: Centro de Investigación y Cultura, Banco Central del Ecuador, 1983- . (Catálogos del Archivo Histórico, 1).

373. Vieira, Cila Milano; Leyla Maria Gama Jaeger; Vera Isabel Caberlon. Levantamento bibliográfico parcial de obras raras e/ou valiosas de Biblioteca Rio-Grandense. Rio Grande: Editora da Furg, 1987. 351p.

374. Weeks, John. Middle American Indians: A Guide to the Manuscript Collection at Tozzer Library, Harvard University. New York: Garland, 1985. (Garland Reference Library of Social Science, 332).

MASS MEDIA

375. Mota, Francisco. Para la historia del periodismo en Cuba: un aporte bibliográfico. Santiago de Cuba: Editorial Oriente, 1985. 192p.

376. Malish, Basil. <u>Seminar on the Acquisition of Latin American Library</u>
<u>Materials. Microfilming Projects Newsletter. No. 29, 1987</u>. Compiled at
the Library of Congress, Washington, D.C. 16p.

377. _____. <u>Seminar on the Acquisition of Latin American Library</u>
<u>Materials. Microfilming Projects Newsletter. No. 30, 1988</u>. Compiled at
the Library of Congress, Washington, D.C. 18p.

MINORITY GROUPS

378. Baeza, Gilda. <u>Contemporary Mexican American Ideas and Issues:</u>
<u>Periodical Sources</u>. Austin: Benson Latin American Collection, The General
Libraries, The University of Texas at Austin, 1987. 3p. (Biblio Noticias,
38).

379. _____. <u>Mexican American Holidays and Festivities</u>. Austin:
Benson Latin American Collection, The General Libraries, The University of
Texas at Austin, 1986. 8p. (Biblio Noticias, 35).

380. Bilsky, Edgardo and Gabriel Trajtenberg. <u>El movimiento obrero judío</u>
<u>argentino</u>. Buenos Aires: Centro de Documentación e Información sobre
Judaismo Argentino "Marc Turkow", 1987. 2 vols. (Bibliografía temática
sobre judaismo argentino, 4).

381. Gomis, Redi. <u>Notas críticas sobre la bibliografía acerca de la</u>
<u>comunidad cubana</u>. La Habana: Centro de Estudios sobre América, 1985. 87p.

382. <u>Los grupos afroamericanos: (fuentes documentales y bibliográficas)</u>.
Bogotá: Consejo Episcopal Latinoamericano. Departamento de Misiones, 1985.
298p.

383. Gutiérrez, David and Roberto G. Trujillo. <u>The Chicano Public Catalog:</u>
<u>A Collection Guide for Public Libraries</u>. Alameda, CA: Floricanto Press,
c1987. 188p.

MUSIC

384. Béhague, Gerard. "Recent Studies of Brazilian Music," Latin American Music Review/Revista de Música Latinomericana, VIII: 2 (Fall-Winter 1987) 292-299.

385. Calzavara, Alberto. Prospecto para una bibliografía de la música en Venezuela. Caracas: Ediciones de la Asociación "Lino Gallardo", 1986. 58p.

386. "Catálogo de la obra musical de Gustavo Becerra-Schmidt," Revista musical chilena, XXXIX: (Jul-Dec 1985) 12-51.

387. "Discografia de Carlos Gomes," Noticia bibliográfica e histórica, XVIII: 123 (Jul-Sept 1986) 251-256.

388. "Discografia de Francisco Mignone," Noticia bibliográfica e histórica, XVIII: 122 (Apr-Jun 1986) 140-143.

389. Merino Montero, Luis. "Contribución seminal de Robert Stevenson a la musicología histórica del Nuevo Mundo," Revista musical chilena, XXXIX: 164 (Jul-Dec 1985) 55-79.

390. "As óperas de Carlos Gomes," Noticia bibliográfica e histórica, XVIII: 123 (Jul-Sept 1986) 222-250.

391. Perrone, Charles A. "An Annotated Interdisciplinary Bibliography and Discography of Brazilian Popular Music," Latin American Music Review/Revista de Música Latinoamericana, VII: 2 (Fall-Winter 1986) 302-340.

392. Turino, Thomas. "Recent Publications on Peruvian Music, 1981-1985," Latin American Music Review/Revista de Música Latinoamericana, VII: 2 (Fall-Winter 1986) 361-375.

PERIODICALS

393. Ballantyne, Lygia Maria F.C. The Alternative Press in Latin America: A Checklist of Current Serials. 26p. Submitted at SALALM XXXIII, Berkeley, California, June 6-10, 1988.

394. Jornais PARAoaras: catálogo. Belém: Governo do Estado do Pará, Secretaria de Estado de Cultura, Desportos e Turismo, Biblioteca Pública do Pará, 1985. 366p.

395. Lozano, Eduardo. Cuban Periodicals in the University of Pittsburgh Libraries. 4th ed. Pittsburgh: University of Pittsburgh Libraries, Center for Latin American Studies, 1985. 114p.

396. Merubia, Sonia. Cultural Journals. Austin: Benson Latin American Collection, The General Libraries, The University of Texas at Austin, 1986. 5p. (Biblio Noticias, 37).

397. Varona, Esperanza Bravo de. Cuban Exile Periodicals at the University of Miami Library: An Annotated Bibliography. Madison, WI: SALALM Secretariat, Memorial Library, University of Wisconsin-Madison, c1987. 203p. (SALALM Bibliography and Reference Series, 19).

398. Williams, Gayle. "New Periodicals," SALALM Newsletter, XIV: 4 (Jun 1987) 15-20.

PHILOSOPHY

399. Fornet-Betancourt, Raúl. Kommentierte Bibliographie zur Philosophie in Lateinamerika. Frankfurt am Main: New York: Lang, c1985. 156p. (Europäische Hochschulschriften. Reihe 20, Philosophie, 158. Publications universitaires européennes. Série 20, Philosophie, 158. European University Studies. Series 20, Philosophy, 158).

400. Paim, Antônio Ferreira. Bibliografia filosófica brasileira: periódo contemporâneo, 1931-1980. Salvador: Centro De Documentação do Pensamento Brasileiro, 1987. 123p.

401. _____. "Obras gerais dedicadas à filosofia brasileira," Convivium, XXIX: 1 (Jan-Feb 1986) 3-18.

POLITICAL SCIENCE

402. Abramo, Fúlvio and Dainis Karepovs. Na contracorrente da história: documentos da Liga Comunista Internacionalista, 1930-1933. Sao Paulo: Editora Brasiliense, 1987. 182p.

403. Barrett, Ellen C. Bibliografía sobre actividades políticas, aspectos demográficos y educativos, 1767-1964. Mexicali: Editorial Mar de Cortés, 1981. 64p. (Colección bibliográfica sobre Baja California, 6).

404. "Bibliografía sobre socialismo latinoamericano," Nueva sociedad, 91 (Sept-Oct 1987) 176-177.

405. Bourque, Susan C. "Policy Versus Politics: Recent Trends in Textbooks on Latin American Politics," Latin American Research Review, XXII: 3 (1987) 245-252.

406. Brazil. Congresso. Senado Federal. Subsecretaria de Biblioteca. Eleiçoes e partidos políticos: bibliografia. Brasilia: Senado Federal, Centro Gráfico, 1986. 110p.

407. "Catálogo bibliográfico e documental do processo político mineiro, 1899-1986," In: Tinha que ser Minas!?: ensaio de político mineira. Belo Horizonte: Museu Mineiro, 1986, 14-44.

408. Ferguson, Yale H. "Analyzing Latin American Foreign Policies," Latin American Research Review, XXII: 3 (1987) 142-164.

409. Gillespie, Charles G. "From Authoritarian Crises to Democratic Transitions," Latin American Research Review, XXII: 3 (1987) 165-184.

410. González Gómez, Pilar and Rosa Pérez Recuero. "Argentina: democracia, modernidad y futuro," Pensamiento iberoamericano, 11 (Jan-Jun 1987) 441-449.

411. Handelman, Howard. "The Military in Latin American Politics: Internal and External Determinants," Latin American Research Review, XXII: 3 (1987) 185-196.

412. Iturrieta, Anibal. "Política y instituciones en Chile," Pensamiento iberoamericano, 11 (Jan-Jun 1987) 471-481.

413. Ranis, Peter. "Deadly Tango: Populism and Military Authoritarianism in Argentina," Latin American Research Review, XXI: 2 (1986) 149-155.

414. Souza, Amaury. "Março ou abril?: uma bibliografia comentada sobre o movimento político de 1964 no Brasil," In: Trilogia do terror: a implantaçao. Wanderley dos Santos et al. Sao Paulo: Vértice, 1988, 193-213.

415. Torres Dujisin, Isabel. "Partidos y sistemas de partidos en Chile," Pensamiento iberoamericano, 9 (Jan-Jun 1986) 456-462.

PUBLISHERS

416. Brazil. Ministério do Interior. Secretaria de Planejamento. Coordenadoria de Documentação. Bibliografia de publicações oficiais do MINTER/Ministério do Interior, Secretaria Geral, Secretaria de Planejamento, Coordenadoria de Documentação. Brasília: A Coordenadoria, 1987. 40, 37, 97 leaves.

417. Sepúlveda, Maria Conceiçao A. Indice das publicações editada pelo CEDEC, 1977-junho 1985. São Paulo: Centro de Estudos de Cultura Contemporânea, 1985. 65p.

RELIGION

418. "Bibliografía sobre religión, creencias y sociedad," Nueva sociedad, 82 (Mar-Apr 1986) 187-189.

419. Callender, Jean A. African Survivals in Caribbean Religion: A Select Bibliography. Cave Hill, Barbados: Main Library, University of the West Indies, 1986. 91p.

420. Castro, Manuel de. "Fuentes documentales para la historia franciscana en América, Archivo ibero-americano, XLVI: 181-184 (Jan-Dec 1986) 111-171.

421. Dodson, Michael. "The Church and Political Struggle: Faith and Action Central America," Latin American Research Review, XXIII: 1 (1988) 230-243.

422. Frere, Penny. Liberation Theology in Latin America. Austin: Benson Latin American Collection, The General Libraries, The University of Texas at Austin, 1988. 8p. (Biblio Noticias, 44).

423. Meléndez, Guillermo. "Iglesia, cristianismo y religión en América Central: resumen bibliográfico, 1982-1985," Cristianismo y Sociedad, XXIV, 3a época: 89 (1986) 91-119.

424. Mota Murillo, Rafael. "Transmisión franciscana de las culturas pre-hispánicas, Archivo ibero-americano, XLVI: 181-184 (Jan-Dec 1986) 331-404.

425. Reyes, Dámasa et al. Bibliografía sobre iglesia en América Latina. La Habana: Casa de Las Américas, Biblioteca José A. Echeverría, 1986. 74p.

426. Ruiz Guerra, Rubén. "Consideraciones acerca de la bibliografía del metodismo en México," Secuencia, 3 (Sept-Dec 1985) 64-72.

427. Soares, Ismar de Oliveira. "Os periódicos editados pela Igreja no Brasil," In Puebla/Brazil: comunicação, um estudo crítico. Clârencio Neotti, coordenador. São Paulo: Loyola, 1981, 104-114.

SOCIAL SCIENCES

428. Arteaga, Ana María. La mujer en Chile: bibliografía comentada. Santiago: Centro de Estudios de la Mujer, 1986. 294p.

429. Ballantyne, Lygia Maria F.C. Women in Latin America: A Checklist of Current Serials. 18p. Submitted at SALALM XXXIII, June 6-10, 1988, Berkeley, California.

430. Berry, Albert. "Poverty and Inequality in Latin America," Latin American Research Review, XXII: 2 (1987) 202-214.

431. Bibliografía argentina de ciencias sociales 1986. Argentine Bibliography of the Social Sciences 1986. Buenos Aires: Fundación Aragón, 1987. 156p. Note: Appears annually.

432. "Bibliografía sobre guerra, violencia y guerrilla," Nueva sociedad, 89 (May-Jun 1987) 191.

433. "Bibliografía sobre la clase trabajadora," Nueva sociedad, 83 (May-Jun 1986) 184-185.

434. Boswell, Thomas D. and Manuel Rivero. Bibliography for the Mariel-Cuban Diaspora. Gainesville: Center for Latin American Studies, University of Florida, 1988. 92p.

435. Bravo Ahuja, Marcela. "La élite política en México: bibliografía comentada," Revista mexicana de ciencias políticas y sociales, XXXII, nueva época: 125 (Jul-Sept 1987) 71-93.

436. Castellanos, Beatriz. Metodología de la investigación social: selección de temas: bibliografía curso postgrado. Escuela Prov. del PCC, UIC y Organización de Masas. La Habana: Editora Política, 1983. 146p.

437. Cohen Stuart, Bertie. Women in the Caribbean: A Bibliography. Part Two. Leiden: Department of Caribbean Studies, Royal Institute of Linguistics and Anthropology, 1985. 246p. Note: Part 1 published in 1979.

438. Comité Estatal de Trabajo y Seguridad Social. Centro de Divulgación e Información Laboral. <u>Listado bibliográfico sobre brigadas de trabajo</u>. [La Habana]: [s.n.], 1984. 8 leaves.

439. Czerny, Miroslawa and Andrzej Dembicz. "Tendencias de los estudios regionales en Latinoamérica," <u>Revista interamericana de planificación</u>, XX: 78 (Jun 1986) 121-137.

440. Del Pont Koclin, Luis Marco. <u>Criminología latinoamericana: enseñanza e investigación</u>. San José, Costa Rica: ILANUD (Instituto Latinoamericano de Naciones Unidas para la Prevención del Delito y Tratamiento del Delincuente), 1983. 350p.

441. Dickenson, John P. "Too Many Trees: Not Enough Wood? A Review of Recent Literature on Brazilian Amazonia," <u>Journal of Latin American Studies</u>, XVIII: 2 (Nov 1986) 409-423.

442. Drake, Paul Winter. "The Buoyant Bourgeoisie of Chile," <u>Latin American Research Review</u>, XXI: 2 (1986) 166-177.

443. Durán, María de los Angeles. "Economía y vida cotidiana en Iberoamérica," <u>Pensamiento iberoamericano</u>, 9 (Jan-Jun 1986) 480-484.

444. Fortín, Carlos. "Movimientos sociales en América Latina," <u>Pensamiento iberoamericano</u>, 10 (Jul-Dec 1986) 480-487.

445. García Colomé, Nora C. and Grisel Castro Nieto. "El tema de la mujer en las tesis de licienciatura en antropología social de la Universidad Autónoma Metropolitana-Iztapalapa," <u>Nueva antropología</u>, VIII: 30 (Nov 1986) 239-255.

446. Giacaman, Mariana y Patricia Sanzana. <u>Campesinado chileno: bibliografía</u>. Santiago: Grupo de Investigaciones Agrarias, 1987. 141p.

447. Gibbs, Donald. <u>Public Health in Latin America</u>. Austin: Benson Latin American Collection, The General Libraries, The University of Texas at Austin, 1987. (Biblio Noticias, 41).

448. Goldsmith, Mary. "Para deshalachar la historia: bibliografía sobre las trabajadoras de la costura, la maquila y de la industria textil," <u>Fem</u>, 45 (Apr-May 1986) 50-55.

449. Inniss, Diana. <u>A Selected Bibliography of Materials and Resources on Women in the Caribbean Available at WAND's Research and Documentation Center</u>. St. Michael, Pinelands, Barbados: Women and Development Unit, Extra Mural Department, University of the West Indies, 1987. 119p. Note: To be updated biannually.

450. "Interdisciplinaridade: bibliografia," <u>Ciência e trópico</u>, XIV: 1 (Jan-June 1986) 85-95.

451. Köppen, Elke. "Bibliografía de movimientos sociales en México: selección de estudios de caso por entidad federativa," Revista mexicana de sociología, XLVII: 4 (Oct-Dec 1985) 261-298.

452. Krawczyk, Miriam. "Mujeres jóvenes en América Latina: aportes para una discusión, Pensamiento iberoamericano, 10 (Jul-Dec 1986) 487-495.

453. Lazarte, Rolando. "Migrações internas e pobreza urbana: perspectivas de estudo nos países dependentes," Pensamiento iberoamericano, 10 (Jul-Dec 1986) 496-508.

454. Mesa-Lago, Carmelo. "Economía de la atención a la salud y la seguridad social en América Latina: nuevas fronteras investigativas y de políticas," Pensamiento iberoamericano, 9 (Jan-Jun 1986) 444-451.

455. Moreno Colmenares, José. "Evolución del estado y procesos sociopolíticos en Venezuela," Pensamiento iberoamericano, 10 (Jul-Dec 1986) 519-530.

456. Paco, Delfina and Virginia Pierola. Bibliografía de juventud en Bolivia. La Paz: Centro Boliviano de Investigación y Acción Educativas (CIBIAE), 1987. 150p.

457. Parker, Dick. "Sources on Working-Class History in Venezuela, 1850-1964," International Labor and Working Class History, 27 (Spring 1985) 83-99.

458. Rawlins, Joan M. The Family in the Caribbean, 1973-1986: An Annotated Bibliography. Bridgetown, Barbados: Institute of Social and Economic Research (Eastern Caribbean), University of the West Indies, 1987. 41p. (Occasional Bibliography, 10).

459. Realidad y perspectiva: bibliografía nacional anotada sobre la mujer en Nicaragua. Managua: Ministerio de la Presidencia, Oficina de la Mujer, 1987. 50p.

460. Sable, Martin Howard. Mexican and Mexican-American Agricultural Labour in the United States: An International Bibliography. London: Haworth, 1987.

461. Sánchez Salazar, Edgar. Bibliografía sobre concentraciones de desarrollo rural, 1970-1980. Bogotá: Ministerio de Educación Nacional, Oficina Sectorial de Planeación Educativa, 1982. 72 [3]p.

462. Santos, Lúcia Maria Gurjao and Carmen Cortez Costa. Catálogo de publicações do sistema estadual de planejamento, 1956-1985. Teresina: Governo do Estado do Piauí, Secretaria de Planejamento, Fundação Centro de Pesquisas Econômicas e Sociais do Piauí, 1985. 80p.

463. Scott, Rebecca J. "Slavery, Population and Progress," <u>Latin American Research Review</u>, XXII: 2 (1987) 215-226.

464. <u>Selected Annotated Bibliography on Conditions in El Salvador and Salvadoran Refugees</u>. New York: Lawyers Committee for International Human Rights, 1983. 7p.

465. Souza, Luiz Alberto Gómez de. "Movimentos sociais no Brasil," <u>Pensamiento iberoamericano</u>, 11 (Jan-Jun 1987) 433-440.

466. Stamos, Stephen C. Jr. "Energy and Development in Latin America," <u>Latin American Research Review</u>, XXI: 1 (1986) 188-201.

467. Steinberg, Kip. <u>A Guide to Available Resources for Guatemalan Asylum Claims</u>. [Boston]: National Immigration Project of the National Lawyers Guild, [1986?]. 8 leaves.

468. Tiano, Susan. "Women and Industrial Development in Latin America," <u>Latin American Research Review</u>, XXI3 (1986) 157-170.

469. Torres de Hering, Lucy. <u>Catálogo colectivo de materiales bibliográficas sobre adolescencia en Colombia</u>. Bogotá: Asociación Salud con Prevención,1987. 240p.

470. United Nations. Economic Commission for Latin America and the Caribbean. Biblioteca. <u>Bibliografía sobre política social</u>. Santiago de Chile: La Biblioteca, 1985. 39p.

471. Valdez, Robert Otto Burciaga and Kevin F. McCarthy. <u>An Annotated Bibliography of Sources on Mexican Immigration</u>. Santa Monica, CA: Rand, 1987. 57p. (Rand Note: N-2392-CR).

472. Verdesoto, Luis. "Ecuador científico," <u>Nueva sociedad</u>, 81 (Jan-Feb 1986) 167-176.

473. Weinstein, Marisa. <u>La juventud en los textos: una bibliografía reciente</u>. [New York]: Center for Social Policy and Planning in Developing Countries, Columbia university; Chile: Facultad Latinoamericana de Ciencias Sociales, 1987. 58p.

474. Edel, Matthew. "Latin American Cities: Recognizing Complexities," Latin American Research Review, XXIII: 1 (1988) 165-174.

475. Gutiérrez-Witt, Laura. City and Regional Planning in Latin America. Austin: Benson Latin American Collection, The General Libraries, The University of Texas at Austin, 1986. 4p. (Biblio Noticias, 33).

476. Kowarick, Lúcio. "Movimentos urbanos no Brasil contemporáneo: uma análise da literatura," Revista brasileira de ciências sociais, I: 3 (Feb 1987) 38-50.

477. Roca Gutiérrez, Jaime. Bibliografía sobre planificación urbana de Guayaquil. Guayaquil: Consejo Nacional de Desarrollo, Dirección Regional; Universidad de Guayaquil, Facultad de Ciencias Naturales, 1984. 2p., 40 leaves.

AUTHORS

SUBJECT INDEX